AM I

THE

ONLY

AM I

THE

ONLY

POETIC COMING OF AGE
HEALING JOURNEY

Desiree M. Palmer

Copyright © 1999 © 2021 Desiree M. Palmer

Published by Satori Publishing
All rights reserved. Printed in the United States of America.
No part of this book may be used or reproduced in any
manner whatsoever without written permission of the
Author and Publisher.

Art by Desiree M. Palmer

www.DesireeMPalmer.com

ISBN: 978-1-7373455-2-7

Dedication

To the boy I loved, but not enough.
You walk with me, still.
I feel your hand, your heart, your strength
I visit you
You visit me
Your feathers remind me when you're near
I know you are always my protector
I Love You

CONTENTS

PREFACE

In those carefree days of homework and high school hallways, my biggest regret was not seeing how one of my best friends was in trouble. My biggest fear was continuing to live by my mother's rules for even one more day. And my biggest dream was to move away and become a fashion designer. The world, as they say, was my oyster. All I had to do was open wide and swallow.

Boy did I!

Still, I lost that friend at 17; It broke me in two. I left home at 19; to start my life. Later realizing I traded my freedom. I still live in the same town I grew up in designing not much more than a Halloween costume.

Like most young teenagers, I feel in love. Rather than following my dreams, I decided to stick around and stay with him. Of course, I came up with all kinds of other excuses and reasons not to chase my dreams, hell, even staying for him was an excuse if I'm being honest. The truth is my own fear crippled me. By the time I overcame my fear, I had a baby, responsibilities, and dozens of reasons I couldn't go do... anything.

Somewhere in between, I had a life. A life that I still look back on and wonder how I made it out alive. That girl was reckless, she was dumb, she was used, she was brave, she was courageous, and yes more than a little alone. Even if she never was more than a mile from someone she knew and someone who loved her.

Not all the words on these pages were from something I personally experienced; some were stories from my friends or family. Nevertheless, they were all stories I wore for a time, long enough to write about them. Then I folded them up and put them away in the closet. I found them in a box and decided it was time to let them fly. Things, stories, experiences, are most useful when we can grow out of them and pass them on for someone else to use for a while. These have helped me, crippled me, kept me warm, and held me... long enough. I must make room in my closet for what is to come next.

I will likely never reveal which are mine and which are others or who each of these is about. My secrets belong to the page now. The healing came with the writing. I give them to you now in hopes that your healing can come with the reading. Wear them, burn them, curse them, love them, do what you will. Find your own voice and speak your truth. Don't stop healing with silence.

This was the first book I ever wrote; I have since written several more, Novels and non-fiction, rather than poetry. The rush of having this one bound and the sight of its naïve prose made me long to finish it. It isn't wonderful. It isn't perfect. Then, neither are we, not ever. Still, maybe that is exactly what makes us perfect. Our imperfections. But we are especially imperfect in our early twenties. Too old to be adorable. Too young to be seasoned. No one even had the decency to tell us outright. They let us figure it out on our own.

So, if you ever find yourself in need of power, borrow mine. And, if you ever find yourself alone, pick this up and read it or hold it and know, you aren't, the only.

– DMP

The pen is my blood, my tongue, my sword.
The paper is my skin, my mirror, my armor.

I Am The Only

Again, I sit alone
With a boulder in my chest
Only having my own bare hands
To wipe away the salty seeds
Of knowing future from my face
Again
I am the only

I Don't Need A Savior

I don't need a savior
I already have one of those
I don't need a knight in shining armor
Fairy tales fade too fast
I don't need a hero
To save me from my scarlet sin
I need a husband who believes
Not, that he simply could live with me
Instead
He could never live without me

Eyes

Two firm perfectly shaped delicate breasts
That's all you see
Although they have dark circles
They aren't my eyes
I do have substance, there's something to me
Do you think they point on their own
Do you think I am empty inside
Look in my eyes if you can
If it isn't too painful to realize
There is more to me
They're green you know, my eyes, they're green
You with your wrinkled sexist skin
Showing truly with which head you think
Never knowing I hold secrets you cannot know
You can never comprehend

SOUL

If I bare my soul to you
Will you take it deep inside
Will you show it comfort
Protect it from the world
Will you use it wisely
Will you know it's worth
Or
If I bare my soul to you
Will you cast it out in hate
Will you throw it on the ground
Burn the love it holds
Will you crush its dreams
Will you show it mercy

Silently I wait
Silently I wonder
What would you do?
If I bare my soul to you

UNTIL THEN MY LOVE

I sit with thundering wonder
Awaiting your beckoning call
Of love or lust or anything
You might offer as payment
A bounty of the love I've given
Without compensation in kind
Show your face to me
If that's all you can give
Your soul being more
Than my meagerness can ask
That all mighty pedestal
Will crumble and fall
I'll be here to catch you
And you falling wondering pride
Aimlessly...
Motionless...
Awaiting your just demise
You'll see me then
For all I am
That your foolishness
Blindly
Couldn't see

RAIN

God's crying so I don't have to
His tears are falling on my eyes and toes
Salt drops for joy and pain
Trying to show me
How
To let go

ADORE ME

Don't you care about my lost dreams
The ones I gave up being your slave
You got your dreams, while becoming lazy
Your neglect shows in the fat you know carry around
your waist
Everyone who sees you knows
I am your foot maid
The chores I wanted to please you with are thankless
They are now expected
Did you see me die inside
Did you enjoy knowing that my internal death would
cause me to never leave you
Wake up you thankless lazy bastard
Wake up and see that I do still adore you
Somewhere inside
Adore me
I'm not your slave
I'm your queen
All I desire from you is love
I need no jeweled crown

DON'T LOOK

You say to show me to you
You want to know me inside
You can't handle me
Be satisfied with what I show you
Don't beg me to disappoint you

SMILE

So
Like every other ball-less day of my life
I simply smile
And go on

Not Good Enough

WEAK STRENGTH

I'm standing strong in my weakness
Until he's gone
It will be much easier then

I MUST

Terrified
I throw myself into the jaws of unknowing
Gracefully
I step into the uncertain force calling me
Knowing only, I must
My childhood held the depth of my future
Convinced I was to be a who
Still that magnet draws me toward that thing
While blurry
Is clearly in front of me
Eyes shut
I leap
With a step too large for me to grasp just yet
If I am to land on the pedestal of all
Or swallowed by a frenzy of feeding animals
I do not know
But
The one truth I have remains strong
After all the weak years past
I must
I simply must

IMPATIENT

I'm not in control of my own destiny
But want to be
I deal with harshness and cruelty with every new sun
I gather to my silent tears by every moon
Curiosity rules my mind and yearns to know when
Impatient to wait my distant gold
Come to me now
Oh, sweet fate
Usher me
Show me the way
The light
My hearts path
Provide me with the blessing of all you hold and
conspire to bring me
Make me no longer wait

I Feel It

I feel it coming
It is near
My heart pounds with anticipation
It flutters crazily and throbs
I move and turn to avoid it
But
It is still coming
Numb and anxious
Every day I feel the nausea
In my belly
The question of what and when
I'm weak to the fight
I don't know the cause
And worse
I don't know the effect
I'm frightened and scared
Unable to control the inevitable
I just know
I feel it
It's coming

How Peaceful

Finally, I'm free
I broke the porcelain walls
And the lovely glass rose
I embraced the terror and overcame the beast
I am free from your so-called love
What torture I thought I would have
Alas, I need not hurt
I gave my heart peace
If I had known, the sword wouldn't hurt
As much as the longing did
I would have been gone long ago

8 SECONDS

He embraced her perfume
As she moaned in a thousand languages
And put a frantic winter to sleep

FLY ON THE WALL

Believe me my love
You are my only hearts desire
I long for your touch
I miss your gentle tongue on my lips
Know I am going crazy because you're not here
Hold on...
Click
Hello?
Believe me my love
You are my only hearts desire
I long for your touch
I miss your gentle tongue on my lips
Know I am going crazy because you're not here
Will you be here soon?
I'll see you in a few minutes
Bye.
Click
Are you there?
Sorry...
So, when can I come over?
I am busy for the next few hours.
I'll see you then.

VACANCY

Come to me in my empty skin
Leave your payment for my destruction
Look over me as if I don't matter
Don't question my closed eyes
Do as you must
It's your dollar...
Now it's mine
It wasn't that hard
I've worked longer and harder for less
I just need to pay the rent
Soul come back to me now
Soul...
Are you there?

SIDEWALK

Laying here on this sidewalk
I'm reminded of you
It has been warm
It provides direction
It is honest
Now it is cold
It is hurtful and broken
It is dirty and covered
I will leave it too
Using it for a single purpose
And then moving on

STILL HERE

I've held your wound
Longer than should be allowed
Daily feeling your affliction
Memorializing your deed
Again and again
Bleeding repeatedly
Why hasn't it healed?
The panic inside
The ache outside
Haven't I been through enough?

LOST FOUND FREE CAGED

I WILL HURT

I will hurt
The distance is far
The is ground is firm
Yet I can't stay here
Gazing over the edge
I see you
Your earth seems comforting
I will not remain safe
If it means being without you
Reluctantly and willfully, I take that step
I close my eyes and lean forward
Though I am falling fast
I am remembering every inch
And cherishing every second closer
I feel you coming near
Opening your arms to me
I know where I will land
I don't fear your surface

BE CRUEL

Don't say that
That is even worse
I can't guard my soul from you
Unless you are cruel
Don't realize I'm lonely
Don't bring me your comfort
Say I'm useless and ugly
Say I'm not worthy of your kindness
Tell me I don't deserve to be loved by you

WHITE VEIL

Sitting with this solitary moon
I remember you
The way you held me
The way you insulted me
You changed your soul
But it was too late for me
She received your goodness
I received your distance
Alone now I see your smile
I see you lift her veil with pride
I don't want your love
I am happy for your joy
But I am alone
And you are not
I left because you wouldn't
Go near that veil with me
So
It's me
It's always been me
Or
Rather
It's never been me

YOUR GONE

Being slapped across the face with reality
A dream held for so long gone
The rush known so well disappeared

LET ME GO

Let me go
Please
Let me go
I'm trying to tell you I need to leave
I love you
Too much
Let go of my lonely skin
Let my flesh fall from your grip
Let me bleed until I'm healed
Let my scars appear
I must go on
But I can't while you're near
I will stay in your orbit
Entering you room at night to watch you sleep
Restless with my heart
Hovering above your bed
Wishing I could touch your face again
Let me go
Please let me go

BUBBLE

This is a strange place
This sphere
No way out
No way in
Going anywhere I desire
But staying where I am.
I go near what things I wish.
But just as it protects me from others harm it keeps
those things away
From my empty heart
It is a loneliness I love
I don't fear
I don't have to fear
Nor do I need to wonder
Though now and then
From time to time
Occasionally I ponder what it would be like
To feel you
To be cut and hurt
To dream in your world
To take your truth and absorb you so deeply
I do... fear

SENSELESS

I was thinking today
How dreadful it would be
If I woke tomorrow
Suddenly senseless to you
No longer able to feel your chest
Unable to kiss your lips with passion
Never hearing your voice in my closed distant ear
I couldn't taste your skin when I cherished your neck
Your beautiful face
Wouldn't brighten my dark lonely world
I wouldn't know you were there
Simply from your scent
What torture I would have
With glory lost to my sensing past
So, touch me now and taste my lips
Gaze into my eyes and whisper in my ear
Hold me close
So, I can breathe you in
For I know tomorrow
Just after the light returns
I will long for you
Alone
With my senseless mind

LOVE ME FOREVER

There is a boundary I cross
When your spirits near
Inexistent reality of a
Cold
Harsh
Unforgiving world
Crumbling outside your embrace
I become empowered with your presence
Suddenly nothing else matters
No storm
Nor rage
Could pull me from you
Cherishing your eyelids with my moist lips
Your fingertips reaching through my being
And touching my soul like no one else
Don't make me go back out there
Keep me by your side
Stitch our hips together
Forever
With our love
Say you won't leave me
Or please
Don't open the door

NOT AGAIN

I remember this feeling
That knot in the pit of my belly
The knowledge of a horror just beyond my teeth
Frantic anticipation
Of what you claim to know
Praying you know nothing more
Knowing there is nothing more
Still, I wonder
What could it be
The last time I had this chill in my bones
I felt a shaking tingle in my veins
I lost my innocence
I became touchable
I also became untouchable
Because that touching was horrendous torture
I still weep from it
Will this be a same

WHO

The way he looked at me
I saw something in his eyes
I felt the call in my soul
With one innocent smile
He made me think I'm beautiful
And important
And comfortable
And worthy of all he can offer
Just by his eyes
What power he possesses
How I long to know him

SCARED

Telling you what I must frightens me
I don't want to hurt you.
But fearing you won't hurt
Frightens me more.

LONG ENOUGH

It's so sad when a heart is lost to the unwilling
numbness
Of an uncaring unreciprocating heart of another
Passion is lost between the sheets
Of what could have been
What never will be,
And dreams that no longer matter
Don't give in to the numb unconcerning ease

YOUR POWER

Just when I lose hope
In this doomed and useless love
Just when I decide to discuss the end
My heart gives into his face
His hands
The power he has over me
Between my legs
Finally, and justly
I decide my worth is more
Than the sum of his calls
And the numerous pleasures he offers my body
And soul
Then with the gentle stroking of his hands
And muscles
I lose myself and to his depth
And think
Maybe so
Forgetting again my worth
Is more than bodily pleasures
And how I longed to be held
And loved
 in return

I'M HERE

I will not go on my knees
To beg a love
I will not get
I will not ignore a past that you will not ignore
I am here for you now
Only wanting your tender soul
I realize your hold on her
That she doesn't share for you
Release her imprinted image from your being
Long enough to feel my heart
Just once
Know me and how long to know you
Bear yourself to me
Before I am no longer here
To be naked in front of

RAPE

Painful you force the bruises on my body and soul
Stop
Please, I beg you
Stop
Close my eyes, close my mind
Remove my soul, remove yourself
Leave me in the filth you have made of me
Go now!
Before I get the strength
To raise my hand in sharpness
And finish you
As you have done to me
And I will force you
To always know my pain

TROPHY

Oh, lovely man where have you been
Joys you share have been hidden with you
I've waited and wanted what you have for me
Long ago I was a trophy
Slowly and painfully the golden layers I held were
stripped away
Leaving me with little more than the disgust in which I
was carelessly discarded
You have given my gold back
Your gentle words and kind nature have shown me my
beauty is still inside
As I cling to your arm your proudness reflects my shine
to all
I am again a trophy
Don't be upset that I treasure that feeling
I also treasure you
You are my golden arm jewel

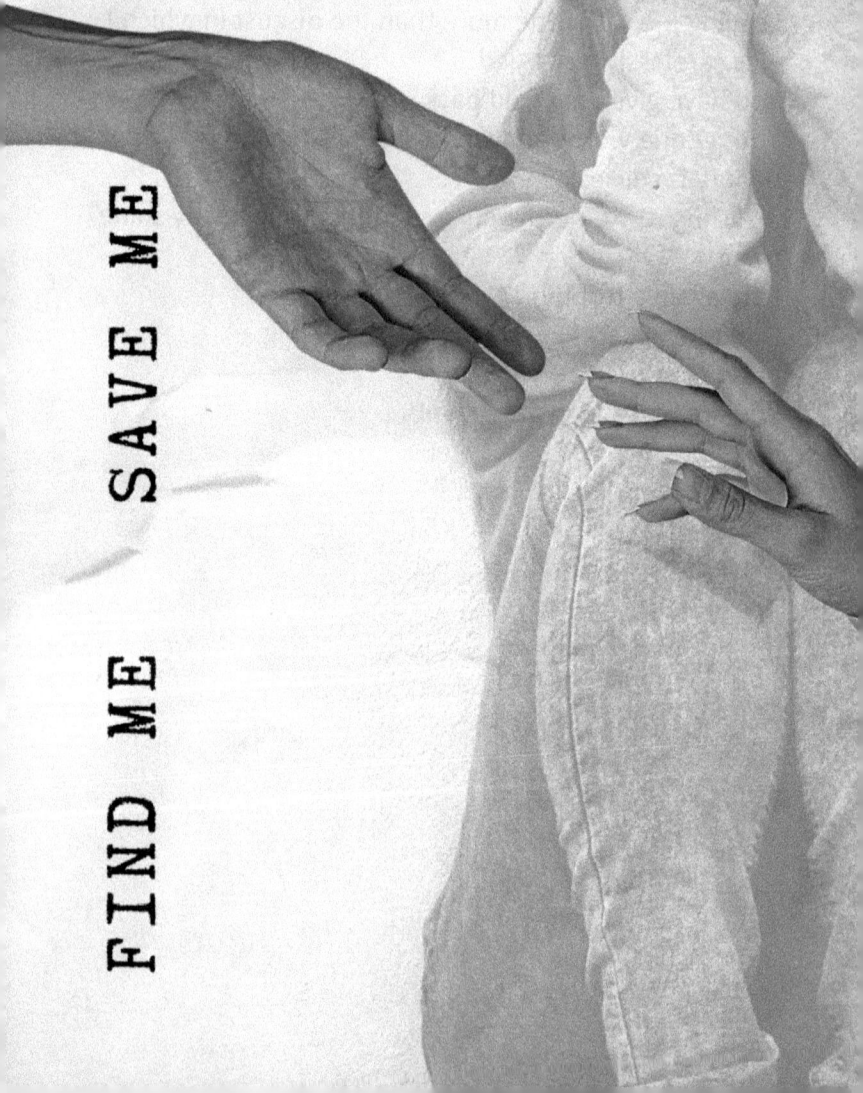

LOVE ME

SAVE ME

FIND ME

You

I had a dream last night
I dreamed that you missed me
And I didn't care
I woke only to realize that I do
And you don't
Just as it was
Before I closed my eyes last night
To dream

INSIDE I SHOUT

From inside I shout
"say it,
Say it,
You fool.
You feel it.
He's right there. So, say it,
Just say it,
Say it before it's too late.
Say it!"

SEXY

He doesn't know my arms
Are holding your memory
So unaware that I see you in his eyes
I close my eyes when our mouths and bodies join
It would be too painful to realize
It isn't you I'm enjoying
I devoured him with such passion
He will never know
The name I say was also yours
I smile when I dream at night
You're by my side
You have filled me with your love
Oh, joyful disease
You so in love with another
That you couldn't hold me in truth
I now share your pain
Of everlasting infatuation and love
For a soul you can't hold
I now live daily with the dread
I will never again know your joy
My bones are weak for your love
My skin is barren and dry
Waiting for your moist touch
My lungs need to breathe you in
My heart is stopped with anticipation
Of your blood coming back
To my veins
I understand your soul's death
And why you can't hold me
Forgive me for believing you had any control

TOO SOON

Be gentle
Be kind
Go very slowly
The stitches are still in
I'm trying to heal
Don't try to enter fully
Not yet
Your compassionate hands soothe my ruptured heart
But it is barely beating
You can't be my life support
I must repair myself
Alone
Please dear man
Be patient
My mind realizes your goodness
It's just too soon for my heart to allow you in

WHITE ROSE

I found the last one in this colorful world
A beautiful
Perfect
Thornless
White rose
The world hasn't destroyed it with its pollution
With its sharpness
Its roots are strong and powerful
How was I so lucky to find it
My messy hands don't deserve to touch that rose
My eyes aren't worthy to look upon it
A power with such magnetism
Has control over me
Drawing me to that pure rose
Forgive my past and let me hold you forever
Please let me care for you
Let me redeem myself through your glory
You are the last perfect man
I beg
Let me keep you

I'M YOURS

Fighting every pleasure you offer me
I try to push you away
But I can't
Mercy
It's too late
I'm yours
You are too wonderful to keep at a distance
Pull me closer
Swallow me
I'm yours
I was too weak to hold up against your goodness
My walls were built to keep you out
But I forgot to guard against loveliness
I'd never had that
Take me
All of me
I'm yours

REFUSE

I refused to fall back into your arms
They held my body too close
I refused to call you on the phone
Your words meant too much to me
I refuse to listen to my hearts begging
The pleading screams through my empty veins
I refuse to learn from our so recent past
It still feels real and too alive
I refuse to live without your memory
The pictures in my mind are my dearest treasures
I refuse to ignore your absence
You're next to me every night in my dreams
I refuse to stop obsessing over you
It's all I hold of you now

SNOWFLAKE

Like a snowflake
I fell on your strong inevitable body
I was there only long enough
To enjoy the comfort
And rest
You offered
Now like that snowflake
You've disappeared
Leaving only your moisture
To roll my cheek

IF I KNEW NOW

If I knew now what I will learn then
I would follow my dreams wherever they take me
I would forget about the boys who forget about me
I would take more pictures
I would keep my friends
I would realize my worth
I would love myself
I would know that every time I tell myself I wish I were
more beautiful, I am the most beautiful I will ever be
again
I would kiss the boy
I would be selfish, just a little more

So Wrong

I never knew I could be so wrong
To think I might   not   need you
I thought I would stop loving you
My arms said I could love him
My mind said I may someday long for him
My heart knew better than they
No one can ever be you
No one will ever be you

LONELY FREEDOM

You are the key
To the lock
On the chain
Around my heart
I'm not fighting to be free
That chain is my freedom

THE SAME AGAIN

I feel every cut of your love's razor-sharp absence
The pain of every vein you sever
Lessons
As you go
Not because I feel it less
But because
It feels the same

THE BALLOON

No amount of pleading brings back that balloon that a
child carelessly let go of
Regretful tears won't return its presence
The same lesson given early
Haunts me now
But you are more precious than that balloon

ACOMPANING PAIN

Why when I love to be lonely
And safe from all possible harm
Do I still long to be touched and wanted
How do you love one and not the other
Love and touch
If you can give up that which brings you pain
Should you not also give up that pains accompanying
pleasure

YOUR SWEET WORDS

EMPTY POWER

The pain of you leaving is now gone
In its place lies emptiness
The comfort of your absence disappeared
Leaving me void and dry
My words no longer have the power
You once gave them

CRUEL

How could I be so cruel
I could hear the pain roll down your cheek knowing I am
the cause of your effect
I pray I must never be judged for this
Such a good dear and wonderful man
You never wanted for this sorrow
I passed on the guilt I have
Something without my control
The unwilling numbness
Of my heart to ever
Love again

OBSESSION

Obsession
Obsession
Say it to yourself
Obsession
The word beckons to you like the product of it
From a passing thought
To a consuming crime
Obsession knows its evil purpose
Still unable to resist
Forward with eagerness
Sleepless nights
Restless days
Over and over
Stronger and stronger
The animal grows
And devours everything in its way
Forgetting conscious feeling and courtesy
Forgetting loveliness and wonder
It's passion feeds on its prey's denial
When the prey wins
As it will
For it has forgotten
The creature leaves sulking
A void in the obsessions place

STRANGERS IN THE NIGHT

You comfort me and know my fears
You share my fears of never lasting love
You have lost the same loves as my heart
I trust you
Because you are so me
I know you must be a safe harbor
Let me come to you to rest
Take me in your arms
And let our bodies drown in each other
Visit my tinder crevices
Show my skin your passions salt
Choose me
Knowing you own nothing more
Let me tie down just tonight
And feel your safe freedom
By the colorful sky I'll float away
Remembering your good deed
You offered your harbor
To my heart
To rest

SATISFIED ALONE

I feel it again
That longing for love
But is it real
Can I trust it now
I never have before
When I finally give in to passion
I quickly flee those comforting harbors
I want that rush with all I am
But will I survive the crash
The pain my obsession of your absence gave me
All I needed
Why must I want for more
I never again want to hurt another soul
Simply for my longing of companionship
Lord give me the power to resist the call
Give me the happiness to be
Satisfied
Alone

HIDDEN MANTIS

Watch out for her
She's deadly
Her vixen eyes will draw you in too deep
Those claws will penetrate beyond your skin
Listen to those who really love you
She has a power over your eyes
She'll make you blind to her malice
Right when you say I do
She comes out
That red eyed slimy goriest creature of a being
She will devour
Your passion
Your soul
Sucking the blood of your every vein
Until all the love has gone
Trust my words
All who know her
You will suffer her wrath
Be sure
Her viciousness need not be doubted

THE LUCK ONE

Count your blessings you beast
Luck is on your side for now
For if I made the rules
You my mantis
Would surely be gone
You aren't worthy of the blood
In your demon veins

WHY

Why do the good ones suffer death
When the beast continues to live and feed

I'M

Longing to touch your well chiseled structure
remembering your words and your gentle tongue
mindless to my daily annoyance and chores unable to
release your thought
Unwilling to wait a night with such distance choosing
only your voice to hear
Haunting my senses with anticipation
Is the lingering of your cologne
Wanting to enjoy the comfort of your chest
Surely perishing without your presence

STANDARD MALE

I'm too addicted to your cruelties
To believe I won't want you
Trying so hard
To ease myself of your uncaring pains
Swearing to never again to be drawn into the harsh rush
you offer
Then
Thinking you may be the one man who is still left
I fail again
Rejected from your heart
But not your lust
So why do I now wait for your call
Knowing better

FINE BUT LEAVE MY HEART OUT

I'm filled with contempt for you
Almost hatred
All you do is call
And I'm dangling from your words again
Lovingly
Why must I be so weak
So desperate
Allow me to be free and uncaring
Do not throw your sweetness in my face
Only to be taken back once delighted
If all you desire is lust
Then don't portray it lovingly
Let lust be lust
I won't deny you
Be bare and truthful
Don't involve my heart

KNOWING TOO WELL

Sleepless longing
Awaits regretfully
Blooming too soon in your presence
Sorrowful ears rise at every chance
Realizing
The inevitable loneliness

SHE CAN BE THE SUN

I'LL BE THE MOON

HURT ME

I fight an unsettling numbness
I want to be hurt by you
Just to know I still can
I give in to your passion's plea
Now I wait your voice longingly
Knowing too well it won't be in my ears
But so
It isn't hurting
My heart is still cherishing a love
A past too wonderful to free
You can't hurt me
You can't touch me
The distance is too far

CONFUSED

Blank
Emotionless
Convincing myself I care
But don't I
Can't I
My guard isn't allowing it
Is that my sign

FOOLING MYSELF

Convincingly I tell myself she isn't real
Still
Her existence is in our realm
I can't handle the truth of her
She holds your heart carelessly
What if she decides to fight for you
I have fallen too deeply into your eyes
Your beautiful words pierced me lovingly
I want you for my own
At night
I long to wake in your powerful arms
The daytime is all I'm offered
We hide from concerning eyes
You say I'm the only temptation you can't fight
Then give her up
Let her heart free
I will give you so much more
Your dreams can't hold my wonders
You haven't known my precious love
I promise you
But
Then
Apparently
Promises aren't meaningful to you

LONELY AND LONGING

Lonely for compassion and joy
Longing for love and touch
Knowing lonely and longing
Is all I have
Desperation takes over inside
I give to the untrue taken soul
Fully believing I deserve my ill gained love
Please soul be true to me
Give me the truth of love and passion
Take the pain and sorrow
Believe I deserve more than half
Bring me my true love
Give up this new forsaken love
Know I am worthy of real love
Lonely lasts forever
If you won't try
Longing lasts forever
If you don't forget

NEVER

Never give in to those condemning souls
The ones who say you won't
Never give into your condemning mind
When it says you can't
Never give in to life's hurdles
They are there simply to test your strength
Never rely on foreign words
If they aren't your own
 they aren't true to you
Look around and find your glory
And
Never
Ever
Give up

IN YOUR ARMS

Ecstasy accomplished
Hold my body
Take my loveliness
Fitting your generous chest
Your arms around me
The twinning of our auras
Sensing that power draws me closer
Feeling as though we're one
Don't ask me to leave
Let me stay here always
Your comfort is an oasis
It lasts beyond the night

KEEP ME SAFE

Scared of the world's war
I want to be held
To be told everything will be fine
That we will all be fine
Why must we fight
Why must I be weak enough
To think we won't
But if we aren't
And if we know we aren't
Please make one promise to me
Hold me while I die
Comfort me
Tell me of your bravery
Love me when we die
Kiss my lips while it's upon us
Keep me safe in your arms

YOU'RE GETTING TO ME

You've brought back that love
Once known but now gone
You know how to speak to my heart
Your pleasures are beyond my dreams
I'm not fighting it this time
You seem to be perfect
You have everything I've longed for
You treasure me as I do you
You don't rely on anyone for your goals
Your laughter brightens my day
You stimulate my mind
In fact, too much
I can't get away from you
I can't get enough of you
I don't feel unworthy of you
You're getting to me

FAKE

What I love about you most
Is that you make me forget to fake

YOUR HEART

I will fill in your heart
The one you wear on your shoulder
It's empty and broken
Like my love is now
I can make it whole
Let me try

I HAVE MANY

Here I sit again
Waiting for you to come around
Flying through your heart
Aloft wings of desperation
Knowing you aren't aware of the adorers
That surround me
Beggars of my heart
They can't see my painful waiting
They all wonder
When they will have a chance
To be my love
Giving you up is all I long for
But I can't
Weakness fills my heart
And body
When it comes to leaving
Then again
There is another
And another
And another
Reason to leave
Reason to stay
Desperate suitor of my soul

TO BE BEAUTIFUL

You look at their bodies
As if they hold a distant desert
Too sweet for your tongue
You look at mine
As if it the taste is too bitter
For your sweet tooth
Following their curves and steps
In desperate longing for touch
Hiding and turning your eyes when I smile
Innocently
World don't tell me I'm fine
I'm not in your eyes
I starved to be your envy
Your passion
Your lust
I feel my body with drugs
And air
To be who you want
Fainting from my hungry lust
I realize
I will never be your desire
If true beauty I hold
Why then am I alone
Why then are there no
Worthy suitors of my heart
No world I am not fine
I am fat
I am ugly
I am lonely
Don't question my actions
While I become what you want

Not until you stop gazing
At the beautiful people
And start loving me
Not until you no longer spend your blood
On pictures
Not until I am
How I am
And you long
For me

FOR SO LONG

Where do I start
I wanted your flesh for so long
I ached for your touch
Knowing it would only be erotic
You satisfied my desire
Once or twice
Holding me in your arms
You made me fool myself longer
Never did you intend to want me
You only wanted to know
I did
I would
You could
Well
I did
I do
I believe you would disappoint me
You could never be all I dreamed you were
And never really cared
I loved you
But you only pretended

LOVE

I WAS GETTING USE TO
BEING SOMEONE YOU
LOVED

I'M WAITING

He's out there
Somewhere
I know he breathes
I don't crave lonely beggars
I'm sick of lustful hunters
I need a real true lover
I need a man
Who can take my heart
In his hands
And be interested in it
I will not settle for less
I will die alone if I never find him
Why should I deserve less
Than these infrequent things I want
Thieves weaken my heart
Give to me and I will give to you
But I am empty from you emotion drinkers
Fill me with honest attachment
Make my eyes sparkle
From your loves rainbow
No more magic tricks with smoke

INVADE MY HEART

You forget I live
Giving the cold of winter to my soul
Then
When you long to fill the sauna of my body
You decide to call
And invade my heart
Telling me you now care
You now want
I fall on your passion
You take over my emotions and play
Circling the maze of my aura
Being careful not to find
The hidden treasure inside
Fearful the golden jewels
Will be too wonderful
I continue again like before
You call once more
Predictably
But this time it's different
This time I know my worth
And I don't fall to your feet
Your matted eyes open painfully
And beg me to see you now care
You again invade my heart
Stop this cruel circle of pain
Love me
Or leave me
But I can't decide
Because
You invade my heart

WHY I STILL TRY

I see the love you have after so long
You still hold hands and kiss
You are each other's treasure
You try to please each other
You care for each other
You are the only unlonely
Reason I still believe in love
I want to have what you have
I want to find my beloved
And for him to know I am his
You are why I still try

EMERALD

I'm an emerald
I hold a garden of gold and black
I am powerful and precious
Rough and jagged

Will you find me?

IS IT TOO LATE

My heart is tangled with you
You soothe my mind and make me feel lovely
But I wonder if you really care
I want you to care
From time to time
I think you might
But more often
Not
I know I'm here only when she isn't
I want to be your who
Who is your only one
I want to feel and know your love undeniably
I want you so much for my own
I want to hold you in the morning
To be in your arms as you sleep
I want to hear your voice
Just because
Heart don't fail me now
Know the truth and where it hides
Show me before it's too late

THE BEST THING

I knew that day
I would have a lot to be thankful for
I knew that day
You were the best thing I would have
Have I ever told you
What your smile does to me
The comfort I feel from it
How you feel against my body
How blessed I am because of you
Do you realize how deep I long for you
Every day
You are the best thing to ever happen to me
And I want you always
I can't pretend anymore
I can't hide behind my fear
You have uncovered my secret garden
You have found your way in

HAVE YOUR WAY

I let you hurt me
Because I'm weak
I may consent
Still, you violate my mind
I swore I would never let your kind in
You shackled my heart
My mind
My soul
You shred it with your emptiness
You are the best I've ever had
I'm too afraid to leave
She called this morning
As I lay in your bed
I pretended not to notice
She was joining you
Before your mattress was cold
My place was again warm
You were delighting her
As you had me
You don't deny this
You don't pretend
And I don't have the power
To believe I'm worth more
So, my fragility screams
Have your way with me

Slow

Desperate anxiousness
Believing in fake love
Just to own love
Giving into lust full pleading
Not knowing it's reality
So obsessed by ever after
You don't look for truth
Realize your worth
Drop your sourness
Open to real true love
Do not be so fast
It will come

Do We

I think I love you
Again
Not that I stopped
I see you with your legion of lovers
It makes me ache for you
I see your treasure
Inside
You know how to make me laugh
But I can't release my hesitation
Scared you won't accept me
Afraid you will
I fear I will fall deeply for you
I want to hold you
To know you
Again
I fear you can give me the love I need
But I also fear
You can't give anymore
They say we belong together
Do we

NORMAL

Sometimes I feel strange and unusual
Not because I'm bizarre
But because I'm not

In My Dreams

I count the minutes
Until I can sleep
Until I can dream
Until you come to see me
You love me
You hug me
You tell me how much you miss me
Those dreams are the only thing I live for
I don't want to wake up
And I also
Don't want you back

TERRIFYING WALLS

I keep you out with my excuses
My reality is genuine
I refuse to change it
Because then I would be a liar
I may be weak and lazy
But it's working
I can't deal with my walls
And the truth they hold
I won't recognize the terror
I will hide outside that room
Always
Stop trying
It won't happen
You won't come in
No matter how wonderful you are
I can't break those barriers

WHY NOW

I found the one
From whom I wouldn't run
Thinking he was safe
I fell
He was safe because he wasn't free
The same reason he was shielded
Is why I must run
Intense longing begs me to stay
Filling my heart
Break
I know I must
I so wish I mustn't
He is all I have wanted
He shines too brightly
No one in my world compares
To his heart
To his body
To his face
His power
His lust
His laughter
Why couldn't it have been sooner
Or later
When he was alone
And able
But then
I would have to run
And I would not have known his glory

You're Gone

I thought it was her
Who held your heart carelessly
I now know
I was wrong
You are the neglectful suitor of her soul
Yet she has no clue of your absence
She's missing your attention
And is unaware
She
Like me
Hangs on your presence
Believing you do care
You are a cold and cruel being
With no compassion
With no knowledge
Of the love and strength of a woman's heart
I want her to know
But I won't speak
You no longer hold my thoughts
Or my prayers
You are gone
Though I know I could have fallen
I see you
Skin an armor removed
How grotesque you are
You have my sympathy
But no longer my love

BURN ME

I'm vulnerable to you
Your touch and thoughts surround me
They engulf my body
Like a lover's flame
Burning my reality
Destroying my will to resist your company
Oh, sweet light
Dear heat
I ache to feel you
Fueling your passion with my body
Giving reason to your existence
Use me
Burn me
Take all of me
Leave me in ashes
I don't want any other to have your power
Take away the chill
Smother my resistance
I lay waiting only for you
Let me pile to be burned by your flame

SLEEP WALKING

TO CLOSE TO THE FIRE

BACK OFF

Your existence causes me pain
I will not let you do this to me again
I have gained strength from you
And your belittling methods
Of which you try to control me
You will not win this one
Will not control my mind anymore
I am precious and lovely
You will not destroy me
I will fight you until I am gone
So, if you want this over
Kill me
You will not have the satisfaction
Of conquering me
You will no longer bind my tongue
Or my reality
You caused terror than one person should face
My sleeplessness was of your product
I refuse to give in to you any longer
Mark my words
Back off
Or I will show you the wrath
Of a woman scorn
I will show you something
You have never experienced
I will show you how small you are
And how much pain I can cause
You will know what true victory is
Because you will see me rejoicing in it
I will teach you one thing
You are unaware

How to beg for mercy
And not get it
Because once I start
And know
I have not yet
I will not stop
Until your great grandchildren
And thier's
Feel my pain
And know the lesson of loss
They will know how to walk naked
And barefooted
Because they will still pay
For your crime

BEHIND MY SMILE

Clueless world
Uncover your eyes
Look behind my smile
See my frown
Love my heart
Open yours

I'M HERE FOR YOU

My dear friend
Know you mean the world to me
You hold my soul
And caress it with your love
You give me your shoulder as my tissue
You give your time to my bothers
I would wash the world for you
And count the days
Until you were happy
There are no boundaries I wouldn't destroy
For you
You are my one true lifelong friend
I love you dearly
And know you do me too
You are the one who could enter my room
Unguarded
You can make me laugh
And cry
You know my secrets in my fears
Know I'll be here for you
I'll take care of you
When the vultures come to feed
I will never leave your side

GET A CLUE

I told you to leave
I want you gone
I need you out
You don't treasure my heart
Or care for my soul
I no longer love you
I'm happier alone
Or at least without you
Get a clue
I said leave
You never had one before
I don't know why I expect you to now
You've always been clueless to me
To my needs
Let alone my wants
So, my dear
Poor
Stupid
Man
Get a clue
And get lost

DEAR OFFICER

I am your captive
You have forced me into your sweet jail
This imprisonment is delicious
Your touch feeds my soul
You still hold my body
Throw away the key
I tried to free myself
As always
When I become close
But you held tight
In fact, tighter than before
You kept your stronghold
And never wavered
I am so weak to you
Your touch and smile
Move me beyond words
I am too far gone
To leave now
It's too late
I love you

USELESS WORDS

Trying to describe your meaning is useless
There are no words
To give that truth
Words I chose have been used in past
They still can't give you life
All my former loves hold you
But still so much more
Consuming my thoughts and air
You drive me to ends I have never felt
So many times, I have believed
This is it
But they were all the same as before
You give such enormous power to my heart
I feel you in every bit of me
My life in each cell of our being
Electric and tingling
You ignite my soul
I want to give you justice
But useless words are all I find
Put your delicate lips to mine feel
My love
And know my truth

YOUR KNOWLEDGE OF ME

You say you know what I need
You realize from where I come
But I doubt you do
I deny your knowledge of me
I have no faith in your eyes
And their power to see inside my heart
Nonetheless, I fall into you in your arms
Giving my heart to the wind
To fly through you
Knowing I will regret my motions
Then from somewhere far away
I hear your voice
Beckoning me
Loving me
I realize
You really do know how my blood flows
The maze of my veins
And the truth I hold
You surprised me
And its joyful
I can only fall further
Catch me dear man
And hold me tight

When I run
Please don't let me go

TELEPHONE LINES

You called today
I never expected it to be you
I had freed me from your chains
My mind no longer bound to your memory
Your beautiful voice struck me inside
I remembered your loving grace
I tried so long to forget you
Why did you have to remind me
I again believe you are my true love
The one for which I will always wait
We visited our past and future
I held on to your every word
Hoping to hear you loved
And needed me too
Waiting to know you always had
But you said nothing of it
Again, I'm left believing you will
One day
Holding your memory
Your joy maintaining
My everlasting infatuation of your soul

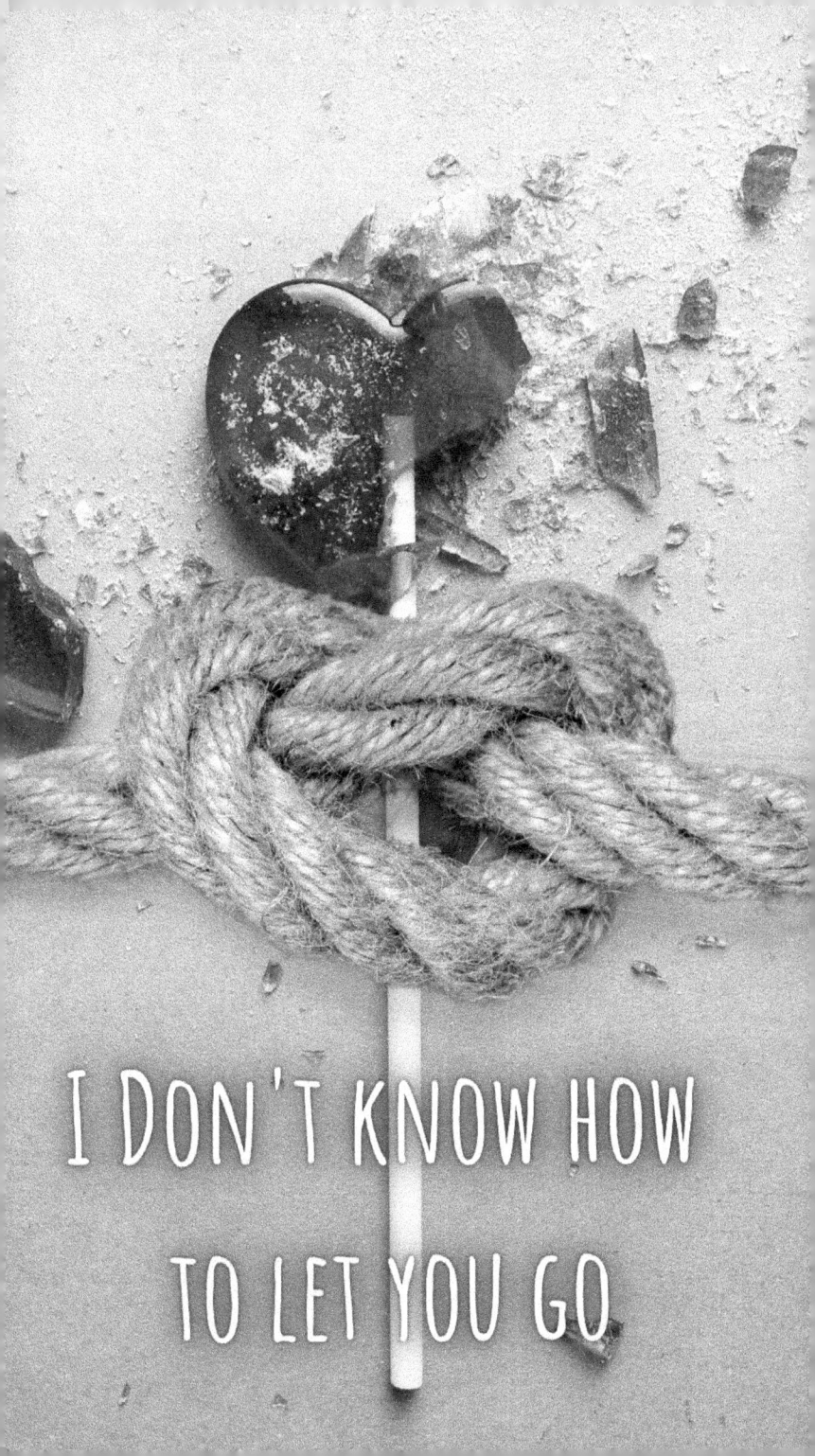

I DON'T KNOW HOW

TO LET YOU GO

YOU AREN'T ALONE

Sometimes you just need to be held
Now and again, you can't be strong
Be weak in front of me
And cry
I won't judge you
Or believe you or less
I won't condemn you for that
I will hold you
And show you love
There are things too large to take on alone
I am here for you
Don't bear your cross alone
Or feel you must
Stay in my arms
Let me help you mend
Cry until you can't anymore
I understand your sorrow
I've been there

I will be here

YOU

I could love just one person
If just one person would love me

YOU II

I want to be more
Than what you leave on the road
There's more to us than casual pleasure
I know you feel it
You get dizzy too

You III

Damn this happiness
I need my anger
It's my relief
Then again
I would give up all the hate inside of me
And its lyrical power
To hold you
No matter my words
I have their past
And their copy to revisit
They can offer my comfort
But I don't think I will need it with you

1, 2, 3, 4

1
My steady
I'm ready
Come to me now
2
Sing me your song
Make me scream
Tell me I am beautiful
3
You know me
You know him
You know I am broken
Come on in
4
It's you again
Where have you been
It's so good to see you
Keep the key

That's it
No more

I JUST ATE

Once again
My eagerness has betrayed me
I'm left wondering if I said
Too much
Too soon
I foolishly believed lies
And read an old untold story
I put words in your mouth
And they came out of mine
How I wish I could hide my truth
I so wanted to keep my love away
A thousand thoughts linger in my mind
They tease my memory and my senses
Dangling their toes in my heart
As if to say
I can't go in
You just ate
You must wait
Not yet

THANK YOU

Protecting the innocent
You put your life to be taken
Thankless deeds of safekeeping
They have taken your freedom
You were left unguarded
Unshielded
Now your life is being sucked away
Now you will not know your son's wife
Nor his life's passion
You will not hold your daughter
You will not wrap around her finger
Or have her tiny ones around yours
You gave so freely of yourself
And now you need to be given to
All that can be offered
Is a simple
Thank you

THIEVES

Wanting to hear those words
Needing to feel they're true
I listened with eager ears
So wide
All your cruel ugliness can enter unseen
My heart is reluctantly sucked into you
I give you your greedy undeserving lust
Once again knowing
You took a piece of my soul
You stole another part of my trust
Slowly you vile creatures are taking everything my
innocence my love my patience my joy my life

DENIAL

I tried to ignore it
I ran from it
I attempted to convince myself it isn't real
I believed they were worthy
In the end you're my comfort
You're my hope
You are my freedom
You're my love
You are the only one I long for
The only one I want to live for
Who I want to sleep beside
And kiss good morning
I've tried to deny it
But I can't
Inside my being you are too real
To simply ignore

WHAT NOW

Confusing ignorance
Unknowing reality
Pleading future
Decide for me
Choose my answer
Faithless in myself
Unconfident with my mind
Unsecure in my heart

DAVIE

Grey
Dry
Stone
Surrounded by others
Engulfed in earth
My mind knows you're not really there
My heart needs to believe you are
I go to you often
Needing your comfort
And never do you respond
Not once have I seen you there
I feel your sweet gentle breath on my neck
Your grace for my trials
Your sympathy for my pain
Though you are no longer here
Nor there
I still feel your love
I'll always remember your face

HOPEFULLY NO MORE

I always said I could leave you
We had a relationship of convenience
We used each other
Equally
I realize now I can't leave you
I've fallen too far
Too hard
I long for your presence and comfort
I dream of you all day
And through the night
I can't let go
I almost told you
I love you
But I know I can't do that
I think you may be falling also
Without confirmation
I will be silent
Praying you aren't still using me
As we did in the start

INNOCENCE

I see now you wish you were
I saw your innocence
In your eyes
Only to believe your eyes lied
But they were true
You want to be innocent
You feel you must pretend
Not to be
You can be
I want you to be

INTERNAL BLEEDING

Swords up
Armor down
My heart is fighting my mind
On your behalf
The sting of your cutting actions
Runs through my veins
Invading everything
I once held true
Everything
I once held pure
My mind is no match to the longing I have
My heart needs a lover and friend
I want to win it all
I'm losing more than my mind
I'm losing my soul
You've taken almost everything
I have no magic potion to make me strong
Each battle weakens me
The war is almost over
Lord give me the strength
To come back
To regain my life
To fight this war
I can't lose again
I've lost too many
To recover
Once more

I was blind
But now I see

MOUNTAIN TOPS

Oh, glorious mountaintops
Take me to your beauty
I once believed my lord was there
I decided to find him
When I could no longer rise
I realized I was wrong
I stopped
And looked
And saw
My lord is there in every valley
In every tree
In every pillowed cloud that surrounded me
He must be there
Nothing evil could make such beauty
Goodness and mercy
Is the only way they could be
I need those tops now
Again
Just to know he is still here
And I am not alone

WHERE WOULD WE ALL BE NOW

Where would we all be now
If black babies came from white mothers
If rich families had poor children
If chauvinistic men turned into women
If soured women were given back their beauty
If we never expected anything in return
If innocence was never lost
If from greed you gained nothing
If none of us could become fat
If we were admired for our minds
If we had everything and wanted nothing
If wearing last year's style made you cool
If no one knew how to hurt others
If anger turned into compassion
If hearts couldn't break
If hatred became unknown
If love was given freely
If we were all the same color
If money had no meaning
If it didn't matter what we look like
Where would we all be now?
If we were all blind
If we were all kind
If we were all truly knew god

OR AM I

Thinking I'm alone
I realized my faults
I'm surrounded with love
And joy
And passion
Friendship too enormous to count
Blindly I held on to lonely freedom
Thank you, dear lord,
You gave me the one thing I needed most
The realization I am not the only
Love inside me
Can never match
Love around me

www.ingramcontent.com/pod-product-compliance
Lightning Source LLC
Chambersburg PA
CBHW071225090426
42736CB00014B/2977